KT-592-153

The BUNTY Book

Printed and published in Great Britain by D. C. THOMSON & CO., LTD.,
185 Fleet Street, London EC4A 2HS. © D. C. THOMSON & CO., LTD., 2010.
ISBN 978-1-84535-415-2

Bunty's most famous friends were The Four Marys. Their schoolgirl adventures thrilled readers from the very first issue in 1958 until the final issue in 2001. Although never renowned for their fashion sense, this story shows what happened to the friends when the fashion revolution of the '60s reached St Elmo's School for Girls.

Serving-maid –
"THE GODS GO
A-BEGGING"

Lise –
"LA FILLE MAL GARDÉE"

Odile –
"SWAN LAKE"

Lilac Fairy –
"THE SLEEPING
BEAUTY"

_bine –
_RLEQUIN
N APRIL"

"SYMPHONIC
VIBRATIONS"

Poor flower-girl –
"NOCTURNE"

Blanche –
"PINEAPPLE POLL"

ER/BON

SOUTH KENT COLLEGE

L08997J0589

STORIES of hardship, stories of success, stories to make you think, stories to make you laugh and stories to simply read and enjoy. The quality and variety of stories was what made Bunty the success it was for so many girls over so many years. And one of the most popular and recurring themes was friendship. Real friends, imaginary friends and animal friends all featured strongly – as did a lack of friends. Many a tear was shed by readers as they devoured the latest instalment of their favourite tear-jerking tale of misery and oppression.

This latest volume isn't *all about* friendship, but it is packed with stories which are guaranteed to bring back memories of friends you have loved and remembered over the years – and also remind you of some you may have forgotten.

No matter what stories were included, it's true to say that, for loyal readers, the weekly Bunty really was a girl's best friend!

Can the girls get out of this dilemma? Don't miss next week's instalment.

Of course, the girls did get out of the dilemma and set to work designing their entry for the great Design a Uniform competition. Many suggestions were discarded as 'too modern' and it was agreed by all that Dr Gull would never allow anything as outlandish as a divided skirt! Trouble was never far away either, in the form of arch-rivals Mabel and Veronica. They couldn't come up with their own ideas, but were determined to foil the attempts of the Marys.

Eventually, however, with help from an ex-fashion designer who had come to live in Elmbury, the Marys produced their entry. Did they win? Read on and find out.

Although fashionable at the time,
the new uniforms were replaced by a more 'traditional' style several years later.

Bunty's number one funny friend was always first for fashion and laughs.

Be My Valentine

February 14th, the anniversary of St Valentine's birth, is the day when girls and their boy friends exchange Valentine cards. There are many romantic superstitions connected with Valentine Day . . .

Superstition said that if a girl wanted to dream about her sweetheart on the eve of Valentine Day, she should remove the yolk of a boiled egg and fill up the hole with SALT. Then the egg should be eaten and the girl go straight to bed without drinking or saying a word—not even "Ugh!"

An old superstition has it that if a girl looks out through her keyhole on the morning of February 14th and sees only one person or animal, she has little prospect of marriage for a long time to come; if she sees a group of two or more, she can expect to be married before many years pass; if she sees a cock and hen together—then she'll be wed before the next Valentine Day!

Here is an interesting Valentine Day custom of long ago. Each lady drew a slip of paper, and the gentleman named on it became her partner for the following year. Some odd pairings were the result of this lucky dip.

In some districts of England, the proper way to deliver a Valentine card was to knock once, open the door, and throw in the card attached to an apple or an orange. The sender had to accomplish the delivery without being recognised—a wise precaution in THIS case!

Five bay leaves, pinned to the middle and each corner of a girl's pillow, will ensure that she dreams of a sweetheart on the night before Valentine Day. And, according to this superstition, the young man will be her bridegroom within a year.

It's a Valentine Day superstition that the first unmarried man a girl meets on February 14th will become her husband. This unlucky maiden should have stayed indoors!

This fun story shows how times have changed – especially when it comes to childcare. Please don't try this at home.

It looks as if things are about to get desperate for the babysitter.

But at least there is one satisfied customer.

Lunch was spoiled by the time the twins were scrubbed clean. As the afternoon continued, it seemed as if Peter and Paula were doing their utmost to annoy Terry. Time after time she had to scold them for misbehaving, and she was glad when at last bedtime came.

THANK GOODNESS— THAT'S THE LAST OF *THEM* FOR TONIGHT.

But the twins refused to sleep—they got up to all sorts of tricks.

Ten o'clock.

I CAN HEAR THEM MOVING ABOUT, BUT I'M JUST GOING TO LEAVE THEM, I'M EXHAUSTED!

WHAT A MESS! I HOPE THEY BEHAVE BETTER TOMORROW.

Next morning.

NOW— EAT THIS PORRIDGE, AND NO NONSENSE.

Oh, dear! Bedtime doesn't bring any relief.

But Terry made the mistake of leaving the kitchen.

RIGHT! NO MATTER WHAT THE BOOKS SAY—

CENSORED

OH, DEAR — I SHOULDN'T HAVE DONE THAT! I'LL *NEVER* BE A CHILD NURSE IF I HAVE TO RESORT TO SMACKING THE CHILDREN.

LOOK AT TIMOTHY.... HE'S LYING QUITE STILL.... HARDLY BREATHING. IT'S A CONVULSION!

RIGHT! NO MATTER WHAT THE BOOKS SAY—

Enough is enough! There's trouble ahead for the twins – or Terry.

Terry wrapped up Timothy snugly, put him in his cot, and phoned for the doctor. A few minutes later, she learned that the baby was in no danger—the doctor said that the convulsion was a mild one, probably brought on as a result of Timothy teething. He complimented Terry on the way she had dealt with the emergency—

This might have bee.
okay in the early '60s, but it's debatable if Terry
would have made a successful children's nurse today

In the early years, the back cover was the place for colourful features. These 'factual' pages alternated with pages of school badges, and there is a selection of them shown throughout this book.

April 25, 1959.

GIRLS of the BIG TOP

Koringa, billed as the only woman fakir in the world, claimed wonderful powers to resist injury. Poisonous snakes, sharp swords and a bed of broken glass were some of the "props" of her act.

This daring young girl on the flying trapeze is Pinito Del Oro. Her only safeguard is her husband below, waiting to break her fall with his body if she should take a tumble.

Jeanette Power would have been sorry if one of these "dancing partners" stood on her toes! Fortunately, the elephants in her famous quartet were too clever to do anything like that.

Mrs Wright, a famous American trainer, was a school teacher before she took up circus work. Maybe, after controlling a noisy class of girls, she found that ordering lions around was easy meat!

Zazel was one of the earliest "human cannonballs." But the explosion when she flew from the cannon was a fake—Zazel was "fired" by rubber springs.

The Countess Bettina de Miremont, a European horse trainer, put on an act that was truly dazzling. She really was a Countess —and she insisted that her horses should be "dressed" in the richest materials, glittering with gold and precious stones.

Kinko doesn't seem to know much about cooking. After the performance, however, the clown will quickly prepare a first-class supper—because "he" is Evelyn King, one of the few lady clowns.

Printed and Published in Great Britain by D. C. THOMSON & Co., Ltd., and JOHN LENG & Co., Ltd., 12 Fetter Lane, Fleet Street, London, E.C.4. Registered for transmission by Canadian Magazine Post.

© D. C. THOMSON & CO., LTD., 1959.

No. 68—MAY 2nd. 1959.

BUNTY, May 2, 1959

BUNTY

EVERY TUESDAY. Price 4d.

" Good job, " Bunty mutters, her face growing red,
" She hasn't got eyes in the back of her head. "
The hair trim went well, till a rash, hasty hack,
Left her poor sister quite scalped at the back.

A pull-out from 1964 told girls what was coming next week. Free gifts were unusual in those days and always caused excitement amongst readers

8 SUPER PICTURE STORIES BEGIN NEXT WEEK!

The dancing life of MOIRA KENT

The heartaches and triumphs of a young girl determined to win a place in the world of ballet.

The CHILDREN'S CHAMPION

The heart-warming story of Hester Langley, a rich girl who gives up everything to help the homeless, unwanted waifs of old London.

The FOUR MARYS

The Four Marys think the Jack Tars are "top of the pops"—and they start up a forbidden fan club at St Elmo's School for Girls.

Wendy ROUND the WORLD

Wendy sees the world as flying nurse-maid to junior passengers of Star Airlines.

Patsy the Pet-Sitter

The hilarious adventures of a girl whose job is looking after other people's pets.

The WILD ONE

At the orphanage, they call Elsie Parkes "The Wild One". No wonder sparks fly when she goes to live with a family of titled toffs!

PHANTOM OF THE FELLS

Maria English comes to Cumberland from Italy—and finds herself ensnared in the mystery of a phantom huntsman!

Sally AT SYLVANO'S

Sally Shaw has the flair to be a skilled window-dresser, but jealous rivals are out to spoil her success at Sylvano's Store.

Now turn over to read the opening instalment of one of the classic stories featured here. ➤ ➤ ➤

If anything unusual has happened to you, write and tell Jenny Wren about it.

In the Furnishing Department, Sally spoke to Mr White, a friendly and helpful salesman.

JUST GO THROUGH THAT DOOR AT THE END OF THE BASEMENT, MISS. YOU'LL FIND A SPIRAL STAIRCASE LEADING DOWN TO THE DUNGEONS.

THANK YOU, MR WHITE.

I FEEL SORRY FOR YOU YOUNG APPRENTICES. THOSE SNOBBISH WINDOW-DRESSERS GIVE YOU ALL THE DIRTY JOBS AND THEY HATE GOING DOWN TO THE DUNGEONS. I'VE WORKED HERE THIRTY YEARS AND NEVER SEEN A GHOST YET.

OH, I'M NOT FRIGHTENED, MR WHITE. THANKS FOR YOUR HELP.

GOSH, WHAT AN EERIE PLACE. NO WONDER THE WINDOW-DRESSERS HATE COMING DOWN HERE.

THE STANDS ARE OVER THERE. I WONDER WHICH KIND OF STAND MISS NEWMAN WANTS ME TO TAKE HER?

Suddenly—

AAAAGH! WHAT'S THAT?

GOSH, WHAT A FRIGHT I GOT! IT'S ONLY A WAX MODEL TOPPLED OVER.

THIS OLD MATERIAL WOULD BE JUST THE THING FOR PRACTISING WINDOW-DRESSING.

WELL, THIS PLACE IS JUST PERFECT FOR PRACTISING WINDOW-DRESSING IN SECRET. MISS NEWMAN CAN'T STOP ME DRESSING OUT THE DUNGEONS!

IT'S STRANGE, BUT SOMEHOW I FEEL QUITE AT HOME HERE NOW. I'LL BE HAPPY AT SYLVANO'S IN SPITE OF THEM ALL.

Sally's trials and triumphs were followed avidly for many months – as wer those of girls in equally 'exciting' jobs, such as teachers, nurses and shop assistants

And there was more to look forward to for readers. Another free gift, another new story and another 'tip-top' book packed with favourite stories and features, all coming soon.

FREE! the Ladybird Ring

"Ladybird, Ladybird, on my hand, Put good luck at my command."

PRESENTED WITH BUNTY NEXT WEEK

THE CHINESE KITE

A present from China brings danger and excitement into Jill Barry's life. This thrilling new picture-story begins NEXT WEEK.

The BIG BRIGHT BOOK for GIRLS!

BUNTY THE BOOK for GIRLS 1965

PACKED WITH TIP-TOP PICTURE-STORIES ABOUT FAVOURITE BUNTY CHARACTERS.

128 PAGES, ALL IN LOVELY COLOUR.

SPECIAL ILLUSTRATED FEATURES TO INTEREST AND ENTERTAIN EVERY GIRL.

NOW ON SALE 7/6d

Look at this great gift for younger children.

Free in Bimbo NOW ON SALE

A "Bimbo" Book for Colouring

This super book has 7 gay pictures to colour with paints or crayons.

Bimbo The jolly picture-paper

Price 6d

Younger members of the family could enjoy a free gift with their copy of the 'jolly picture-paper' Bimbo. At 6d, this publication cost a penny more than Bunty.

The much loved cut-out wardrobe was given room to shine in the annual publications. They weren't popular with everyone, however, and story has it that one couple filed for divorce following an argument over whether or not to allow their daughter to cut pages from a book.

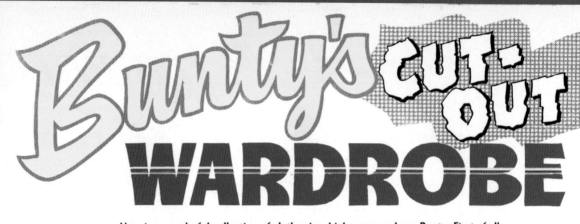

Bunty's CUT-OUT WARDROBE

Here is a wonderful collection of clothes in which you can dress Bunty. First of all, paste the figure on to a piece of thin cardboard and cut round the outside lines. Next cut out all the colourful outfits, taking care to include the white tabs. Now you can fit on the outfits by folding the tabs round Bunty. You can have hours of fun playing with these lovely dresses, deciding which makes Bunty most attractive.

One of Bunty's most endearing characters was Dora Spoone. No matter what poor Dora tried to do, it invariably went wrong – often with hilarious results for both her friends and enemies.

DOPEY DORA
THE HOPE OF THE SCHOOL

DORA SPOONE was the dimmest pupil at Eversford School, so it came as a shock when the school's computer picked her as the most brilliant scholar! As a result, Miss Rockshaft, the Headmistress, had entered Dora and five other clever pupils for the School of the Year Contest — and so far it had been Dora's blundering efforts which pulled them through to win! Now it was time for the gym display and Dora's team-mates, who wanted rid of her, had made a plan. Because of their scheming, Dora thought it was Friday and not Saturday and she was preparing to set off for school while her team-mates prepared to go to Puddledock School for the display.

I DID WHAT YOU ASKED, AND DELIVERED THAT COPY OF YESTERDAY'S PAPER TO THE SPOONES' HOUSE.

AND LOOK—THERE'S DORA GOING OFF TO SCHOOL! WE'VE REALLY CONVINCED HER THAT TODAY IS FRIDAY, AND NOT SATURDAY, THE DAY OF THE CONTEST!

SOMEONE HAD BETTER RUN AND WARN DAPHNE THAT SHE'LL BE NEEDED IN THE TEAM, AFTER ALL!

OH, NO! DORA'S GONE DASHING OFF WITHOUT HER BREAKFAST. SHE'S SO FORGETFUL!

SHE'S ALSO FORGOTTEN IT'S SATURDAY, BY THE LOOK OF THAT BULGING SCHOOL SATCHEL. HOW ON EARTH OUR DAUGHTER MANAGES TO BE SO DIM, I'LL NEVER KNOW!

THE COMPUTER THAT PICKED ME OUT AS A GENIUS WAS SPOT ON! WHEN I WENT TO DO THURSDAY'S HOMEWORK LAST NIGHT, I FOUND I'D ALREADY DONE IT. I THINK I'M GOING TO LIKE BEING A GENIUS!

GOSH! AM I LATE AGAIN? WHERE IS EVERYONE?

THEY'VE GONE! THERE'S NOT A GIRL OR A TEACHER LEFT!

WHAT ARE YOU DOING HERE, MISS? IT'S SATURDAY, YOU KNOW. SHOULDN'T YOU BE AT PUDDLEDOCK SCHOOL, CHEERING ON THE EVERSFORD TEAM?

SATURDAY? OH, NO! OF COURSE I SHOULD BE CHEERING ON THE TEAM!

WHAT AM I SAYING? I AM THE TEAM! THEY CAN'T MANAGE WITHOUT ME!

THOSE POOR GIRLS MUST THINK I'VE LET THEM DOWN! THE HEAD WAS RELYING ON ME TO GIVE THE TEAM A BIT OF SPARKLE.

I THOUGHT THIS SHORT CUT ACROSS THE COMMON WOULD HAVE SAVED TIME, BUT IT'S LIKE TRYING TO WADE THROUGH TREACLE. THOSE POOR GIRLS WILL BE FRANTIC WHEN THEY DISCOVER I HAVEN'T TURNED UP!

But, at Puddledock School—

WE'VE DONE IT. WE'VE GOT DORA OUT OF THE DISPLAY TEAM!

YOU'LL HAVE TO TAKE HER PLACE, DAPHNE.

THE HEAD IS HOPPING MAD WITH DORA!

Meanwhile, outside the school—

THAT WAS A MUDDY RIDE. I NEED WINDSCREEN WIPERS ON MY SPECS!

JUST ONE MOMENT! YOU CAN'T WALK IN HERE, YOU KNOW. THERE'S A CONTEST ABOUT TO TAKE PLACE.

The BEST OF LUCK AND HOW TO GET IT!

To make sure her wish is granted, this girl has walked two miles round Chester's old city wall and is now in the process of running up and down the famous Wishing Steps. Her wish, no doubt, will be a bath to relieve her aching feet.

The legend of the St Keyne well in Cornwall states that the husband or wife who first drinks its water will rule the household. You can understand this man's hurry, but it looks as if he is too late.

The girl going through this contortion is about to kiss the Blarney Stone, set in the battlements of Blarney Castle in Eire. I'm sure her greatest wish will be that her friend holds on tightly for there is a drop of 200 feet below.

You don't often see children throwing away their hard-earned pocket money like this. The reason for it here is simple. It is considered to be very lucky when crossing the Forth Bridge to throw a coin into the river.

Visitors who wish to return to Rome will have their wish granted if they throw a coin into the famous Fountain of Trevi. Those who think this is an excellent superstition are the urchins of Rome who fish out the coins after the visitors have gone.

This back cover feature from the 1960s was colourful and fun. Don't know if any of the ideas worked, though.

The Language of Flowers

Did YOU know that flowers have a special meaning all of their own?

Acacia—*friendship.*

Almond Blossom—*encouragement.*

Aloe—*grief.*

Anemone—*soul of goodness.*

Apple Blossom—*you are preferred.*

This feature from the first ever Bunty Book is a good example of the style popular with readers of the time. It would be surprising if anyone wanted to wear a sprig of heather after reading this, though.

Bluebell—*true and tender.*

Buttercup—*homeliness.*

Calceolaria—*don't be jealous.*

Red Carnation—*my heart is broken.*

Celandine—*don't be downhearted.*

Chrysanthemum—*hope springs eternal.*

Cornflower—*never despair.*

Daffodil—*welcome.*

Dahlia—*gracious.*

Foxglove—*deceitful.*

Fuschia—*fickleness.*

Geranium—*warm regard.*

Heather—*I am lonely.*

Honeysuckle—*devotion.*

Iris—*have faith in me.*

Jasmine—*friends only.*

Lilac—
unadorned beauty.

Lobelia—*unselfishness.*

Marigold—*honesty.*

Nasturtium—*optimism.*

Pansy—*tender thoughts.*

Poppy—*forgetfulness.*

Red Rose—*love.*

Sweet William—
pleasant dreams.

Verbena—
you have my confidence.

Wallflower—*loyalty in friendship.*

BUNTY CLUB CORNER

★ HERE IS ANOTHER CHANCE FOR ALL CLUB MEMBERS TO WIN A LOVELY PRIZE!
YU MKZ HAYE!

Puzzles played a big part in early reader participation. These puzzles are from the Club Corner pages and offered lovely prizes for successful readers. Getting the answers right wasn't the only important thing, though, as the special note at the bottom of the page points out.

HOW MANY Bs?

HOW MANY THINGS IN THIS PICTURE BEGIN WITH THE LETTER B? BRACELET & PENDANT SETS WILL BE AWARDED TO THE 10 READERS WHO SEND IN THE BEST LISTS.

QUICK CROSSWORD

Dainty manicure sets are waiting for the 10 club members who submit the neatest, correct solutions to this crossword puzzle.

ACROSS:—4 Grizzly animal? 5 Pig's home. 6 Country Africa. 8 Coin. 11 Part of a fish. 12 Fine material.
DOWN:—1 Limb. 2 Colour of grass. 3 Halt, 7 Noma 9 Wicked. 10 Not new

SPOT THE MISTAKES

Can you spot the ten deliberate mistakes our artist has made in this picture? Beautiful scarves in authentic Scottish tartan are waiting for the ten club members who send in the neatest postcards listing the errors.

NOTE—The Editor will judge these competitions. Neatness will count and his decision will be final.

WHO IS SHE?

This tennis star has played in Britain's Wightman Cup team. Beautiful bracelet and pendant sets will be won by the ten club members who send in the neatest postcards giving her name.

WHO IS HE?

British comedian has been the star of many films. Dainty Manicure Sets will be awarded to the ten club members who send in the neatest postcards giving his name.

COSY CORNER

These tricky puzzles from early Cosy Corner pages certainly tested the eyesight of the readers — although no prizes were on offer this time. The 'challenge' was considered prize enough.

SPOT THE MISTAKES

Lovely brooches will be won by the ten club members who can find the most deliberate mistakes in this picture.

There are ten deliberate mistakes to be found in each of the pictures. Obviously a puzzle for young eyes — or borrowing Jenny Wren's magnifying glass.

ALL ANSWERS IN THE BUNTY SECRET CODE, AND ON POSTCARDS PLEASE, TO—

CLUB CORNER (44),
"BUNTY,"
12 FETTER LANE,
FLEET STREET,
LONDON, E.C.4.

Although friends and friendship were central to many story plots, loneliness and a lack of friends and family was another theme which was often in evidence.

★ Anne runs away to avoid going to the orphanage ★

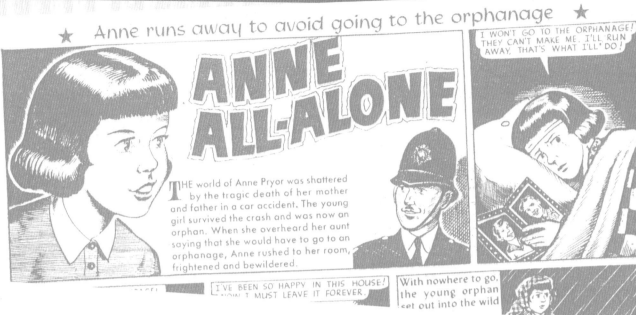

ANNE ALL-ALONE

I WON'T GO TO THE ORPHANAGE! THEY CAN'T MAKE ME. I'LL RUN AWAY, THAT'S WHAT I'LL DO!

THE world of Anne Pryor was shattered by the tragic death of her mother and father in a car accident. The young girl survived the crash and was now an orphan. When she overheard her aunt saying that she would have to go to an orphanage, Anne rushed to her room, frightened and bewildered.

I'VE BEEN SO HAPPY IN THIS HOUSE! NOW I MUST LEAVE IT FOREVER.

With nowhere to go, the young orphan set out into the wild

★ A pleasant change for Lucy— she's living in the lap of luxury ★

Lonesome Lucy

THE year was 1940 and Britain was at war with Germany. Young Lucy Mortimer, still without news of her missing mother, was spending a holiday at Nurse Garfield's home in the country. On her arrival, Lucy, who assumed the name of Sally Dobbing, was amazed to find that Nurse Garfield was the daughter of a Duke—

THIS WILL BE YOUR ROOM FOR AS...

IF YOU WANT ANYTHING JUST RING...

> The stories shown here were typical of those which found favour with readers of all ages. From orphans to those merely separated from their families, all the girls had heartbreak and hardship to overcome before their story reached its happy ending.

★ Linda has her first taste of school life—and detests it! ★

THE LONELY LIFE OF Linda Brown

ORPHAN Linda Brown was a lonely child, for her grandmother was much too busy to shower attention on her. But she had made one good friend in Pat Roberts, a governess. Unfortunately, however, Pat had decided to get married and Linda was to be sent to a boarding school.

BRANDON COLLEGE FOR GIRLS

SORRY I CAN'T COME TO THE STATION WITH YOU, BUT I HAVE A MOST IMPORTANT MEETING. I HOPE YOU'LL BE HAPPY AT BRANDON COLLEGE.

A few hours later. Linda stepped off the train at Brandon Junction.

EXCUSE ME, COULD YOU HELP ME, PLEASE — I'M NEW AND....

One Bunty heroine who knew all about loneliness was Lorna Drake. Life was continually hard for the budding young ballerina – especially when her only friend was in danger of having to give up dancing.

Dancing brings happiness for Lorna—and heartbreak for her chum.

"THE FIRST BALLET DANCERS WERE THE COURTIERS OF KING LOUIS XIV. IN FRANCE. THE MEN'S TIGHT DOUBLETS AND THE WOMEN'S BONED BODICES MADE THEM STAND ERECT AND HOLD THEIR ARMS AWAY FROM THEIR BODIES. THE CLOTHES CHANGED IN TIME, BUT THE WAY OF DANCING DIDN'T."

A GOOD ANSWER, CHILD.

SHE'S PLEASED WITH ME. THIS MIGHT BE A GOOD TIME TO ASK ABOUT THE OPERETTA.

MISS MAYNE — WILL I BE ALLOWED TO DANCE IN THE SCHOOL OPERETTA? MISS HAMPTON WANTS TO KNOW BY TOMORROW!

I'LL TELL YOU THIS AFTERNOON, AFTER I'VE SEEN HOW YOU DANCE IN THE OPERETTA SEQUENCE.

So, when Lorna took her place in the ballet studio after lunch, she was determined to put up a good show. The ballet sequence took up only five minutes of the operetta's time—but Thelma Mayne kept Lorna practising it for two hours!

I HOPE LORNA IS ALLOWED TO APPEAR IN THE OPERETTA. SHE'S TRYING SO VERY HARD TO PLEASE THELMA.

STOP, LORNA!

THAT LAST PART WAS SLOPPY! DO IT AGAIN — AND LET ME SEE YOUR CHIN FLICK ROUND DURING EVERY PIROUETTE.

I MUST GET IT RIGHT!

AH! THAT'S BETTER, LORNA. THE FLICK OF THE CHIN MAKES ALL THE DIFFERENCE IN THE WORLD. THAT'S ENOUGH FOR TODAY.

— AND YOU CAN TELL MISS HAMPTON THAT YOU'LL BE DANCING ON PARENTS' NIGHT.

OH, MISS MAYNE — THANK YOU EVER SO MUCH!

Lorna enjoyed the next three weeks at school. There were rehearsals for the operetta, "The Gypsy's Spell"—there were costumes to be made in the needlework class—the girls all helped in the construction and painting of stage fittings. Then, a week before the performance, Thelma Mayne gave the dancers their first rehearsal in costume.

WHEN LORNA PIROUETTES OFF-STAGE AT THE END OF HER BALLET SEQUENCE, THE REST OF YOU BEGIN TO DANCE ROUND THE FIRE. WE'LL USE THIS CUSHION TODAY —

*A good story — **and** a lesson on the history of ballet. What more could a girl want?*

Ballet lovers may remember this wonderful feature from 1961. Many readers learned facts that stayed with them all their lives by reading their weekly Bunty or pouring over the pages of the latest book.

The GREAT PAVLOVA

NONE of you will have ever seen Pavlova dance, yet nearly thirty years after her death, her name is still a household word. Many people still consider her to be the greatest ballet dancer ever.

Anna Pavlova was born in St Petersburg, in Russia, in 1882, the daughter of a poor washer-woman. At the age eight, Anna saw her first ballet performance and from then on she determined to become a ballet dancer herself.

She pleaded and pleaded until she got her mother's permission, and at the age of ten she was admitted to the Imperial Theatre School.

Dancing was in Anna's blood and she quickly rose to be one of Russia's prima ballerinas. In 1907 she went on her first world tour and was acclaimed in every theatre where she danced.

Pavlova had a mad passion for shoes. She could not resist a tempting pair and she owned hundreds.

In 1917, after the Russian Revolution, Pavlova made her home in England. She kept two pet swans in her garden and by careful study she was able to transmit their grace to her dancing. "The Dying Swan," the ballet excerpt she made most famous, was especially arranged for her as far back as 1905.

Like many great artistes, Pavlova was very temperamental, and she lost many leading men because of this. On one occasion, in full view of the audience, she slapped her leading man on the face when he let her fall.

Besides being a great dancer, Pavlova was also an excellent teacher. When she was not away on tour she spent most of her spare time auditioning and teaching young girls in her own home at Hampstead.

Pavlova was superstitious and was very distressed when, at the end of 1930, a fortune teller warned her of an approaching calamity.

The prophecy was borne out in January of the following year Pavlova was at the start of another tour when her train was involved in a collision near Dijon, in France. No one was hurt, but Pavlova and her company were stranded for several hours.

Pavlova contracted a chill and was ordered to bed when she reached The Hague. The chill developed into pneumonia and Pavlova died there on January 23, 1931, while still at the height of her career

Many long-running characters changed 'appearance' over the years – sometimes because of a change of artist, and sometimes as a result of 'updating' or 'modernising'. In the story shown here, another of Bunty's favourite ballerinas, Moira Kent, looks very different from the girl who first danced across the pages of the magazine.

All too soon the mystery was solved and, thanks to Moira, a reclusive ballerina found the strength to go back to the stage and the kidnapped dancers were released. A happy ending all round.

Different sports were featured over the years. No doubt this spread from the 1970s inspired many a girl to pick up a racket and try her hand at tennis.

TENNIS –

A game resembling modern day squash was very popular with monks in the middle ages.

At times, attempts were made to put down the game because of the disorder often created. Edward III banned it in favour of archery.

The sixteenth century saw the development of courts, enclosed by four walls and containing special obstacles. A more recognisable racquet had also evolved and this game, known as "real" or "royal" tennis, had, as its name suggests, many royal patrons, including Henry VIII, who had a court built at Hampton Palace.

Henry VIII also left a lasting memorial to the game in the form of "service"—a servant used to perform the task of striking his first ball.

1886

These well-corseted ladies are typical of the period.

1905

May Sutton, an American, caused a sensation when she rolled up her sleeves—but she won the title!

1914

Even at this late day, long skirts were a necessity for tennis.

By the eighteenth century, the game had fallen from popularity but a revival in the nineteenth century came from within the universities—and under auspices of the All-England Croquet Club! The popularity of croquet declined as tennis grew in stature and in 1869 Major Walter Wingfield laid down the basic framework of rules by which we recognise lawn tennis today.

In 1875, a code of laws and court size was laid down and two years later, present day scoring was adopted in its entirety. Up till that point, the courts were of no fixed size—some were oval or shaped like an hour glass and rules were non-existent. Some courts even had trees growing on them!

The first Women's All-England Championship was held in 1884 and the first winner was Miss M. Watson. The first great woman exponent was Miss Lottie Dod, a child wonder, who adopted a smash shot, hitherto unknown in women's tennis. This brought to an end the marathon four or five hour matches which involved little more than "patting" the ball back and forward over the net.

Since 1877, the world's top players have competed annually at Wimbledon, the championships with the most tennis prestige internationally. All the greats, such as Maria Bueno, Margaret Smith, Billy-Jean King and Evonne Goolagong have played there—and won!

1927

By then, skirts were shorter, though the dresses had a sack-like appearance.

1949

By 1949, fashions had changed remarkably and even shorts made an appearance, causing a great outcry!

1970s

Now, women's tennis fashions are free and light—and sometimes even a splash of colour interrupts the regulation white!

Now turn over to read about one of Bunty's most memorable tennis stars.

Meet Barbie Mason – a tennis star with lots of talent and lots of problems.

Underhand tactics bring defeat for Barbie!

BASE-LINE BARBIE

CRIPPLED Barbie Mason had worked out a method of playing tennis from the base-line and avoiding running whenever possible. When Barbie and her friend, Rae, were invited to Patricia Clegg's home, it became obvious why the ambitious Patricia wanted Barbie there.

MR TRENCHARD'S A SELECTOR FOR THE COUNTY TENNIS TEAM! PATRICIA HOPES TO MAKE HER TENNIS LOOK GOOD—AT YOUR EXPENSE, BARBIE.

DON'T WORRY ABOUT ME, RAE. I'LL GIVE AS GOOD AS I GET!

Barbie spun her racquet for choice of ends—

ROUGH! OH—YOU SERVE, BARBARA.

WITH THE SUN FULL IN MY EYES! BY THE TIME WE CHANGE ENDS, THERE'LL BE MORE SHADE FOR PATRICIA.

Despite the glare, Barbie served well—

ANOTHER ACE! PATRICIA LOOKS FURIOUS!

IT'S FORTY-LOVE TO HER. SHE MAY HAVE THE WHIP HAND WITH HER SERVICE GAME, BUT WAIT TILL I START USING THE COURT!

THIS TIME—JUST OUT OF HER REACH.

NO USE MAKING AN UNDIGNIFIED SCRAMBLE. I'LL LET IT GO!

THAT GIRL IS LAME! HER LEG DRAGS BADLY—YET, SHE'S AN EXTREMELY CAPABLE TENNIS PLAYER!

On court, the girls fought on —

PATRICIA'S TURN TO FACE THE SUN. LET'S SEE HOW WELL SHE DOES.

Patricia's first serve went into the net. Then—

OUT!

WHAT DO YOU MEAN? IT WAS IN BY A MILE! YOU SAW IT, MR TRENCHARD.

A Bunty Club entry form appears on Page 12.

Test your wits with the "Tricky Teasers" on Page 8.

Patricia won the set 6-4—according to her scoring.

THAT'S IT! I'VE WON. WELL, MR TRENCHARD. HOW ABOUT THE COUNTY TRIALS?

WELL, I'VE CERTAINLY SEEN STAR MATERIAL HERE TODAY, PATRICIA.

BUT NOT YOU, I'M AFRAID, PATRICIA—THIS GIRL!

YOU CAN'T BE SERIOUS! THAT CRIPPLE? AND I WON, DIDN'T I?

SO YOU SAY, PATRICIA. BUT THIS GIRL HAS TREMENDOUS STAYING-POWER. WEARINESS, WRONG DECISIONS—NOTHING BOTHERS HER!

THANKS, MR TRENCHARD. BUT YOU CAME TO SEE PATRICIA. WE'D BETTER GO NOW.

HER NAME'S BARBIE MASON—IT'S ALWAYS BEEN HER AMBITION TO PLAY FOR THE COUNTY.

YOU KEEP OUT OF IT, RAE JAMES! OH, WHY DID I ASK YOU TWO TO COME HERE?

Next morning—

I FEEL HEAPS BETTER AFTER A GOOD SLEEP. THAT TROUBLE OVER PATRICIA DEPRESSED ME LAST EVENING. I WONDER IF MR TRENCHARD WILL WRITE TO ME?

GOOD MORNING, DEAR. BREAKFAST IN BED FOR YOU! YOU LOOKED SO WEARY LAST NIGHT.

YOU SPOIL ME, MUM. ONE WONKY LEG DOESN'T MAKE ME AN INVALID!

YOU MUST REST ALL YOU CAN.

I KNOW. RESTING MAKES ME ALL THE FITTER FOR TENNIS.

I HAVEN'T TOLD MUM ABOUT MY COUNTY HOPES, YET.

Barbie's ambition knew no bounds and readers had no doubt that eventually her dreams would come true. Several months later —

I'LL KEEP BOTH FEET ON THE GROUND, EVEN IF ONE OF THEM IS TWISTED AND USELESS. IT'S A LONG WAY TO CENTRE COURT—BUT I'LL GET THERE ONE DAY!

The End

Pancake Day Parade

This is a present-day custom connected with Pancake Tuesday. Every year, housewives run a race through the streets of Olney, in Buckinghamshire, with a pancake in a pan. This pancake has to be tossed three times during the race. Many other customs connected with Pancake Tuesday have been long forgotten, however. Here are some of them—

The Pancake Bell was rung early on the morning of Pancake Tuesday, to let housewives of old know it was time to mix the batter and get their frying pans sizzling!

February brings Pancake Day – and another fun-filled feature for Bunty readers. Does anybody know any of the songs mentioned below? Answers on a postcard please – but no prizes!

It was the custom for all members of the family to take part in a competition to find out who could toss a pancake highest—and catch it in the frying pan again, of course!

An old superstition held that, if you wished to have money in your purse all year round, you should eat pancakes on Pancake Tuesday and grey peas on the following day.

In some country districts, the clamour of a bell brought the local children running to take part in a scramble for pancakes, which were dropped to them from the belfry.

It was an old-time rule that the last member of the household to be seated at breakfast should be first to receive a pancake. The intention was that the sleepyhead would be shamed into getting up earlier in future!

Girls and boys of bygone days used to go round the doors singing special Pancake Tuesday songs. Their reward was a helping of pancakes and other tasty morsels baked by the housewives.

★ Lindy gives a thoughtless dog-owner a piece of her mind ★

LINDY MARTIN

The Animals' Friend

THE annual Carnival Week was a big event in the town where Lindy Martin lived. There were dances and processions, and a fair visited the town. The highspot of the week was a grand ball at which the Carnival Queen was crowned. The whole affair was organised by students from the local university in aid of various charities.

Lindy worked for the A.P.S., and her job was to go to the help of any animal in trouble.

Lindy knew several of the students, and one of them, Tony Richardson, tried to persuade her to send in her photograph for the Carnival Queen competition.

"What, like this?" laughed Lindy.

She was wearing the jumper and slacks in which she usually worked.

"You'd be all right, smartened up a bit," said Tony.

"Thanks!" said Lindy.

"You know what I mean," said Tony. "You're equal to any of the entries we've got so far."

He showed Lindy the photographs that girls had sent in. They had all been taken in very glamorous poses. Lindy was struck by one that showed a girl in a slinky evening gown. She was posed with a large, silky-haired dog.

"That's nice," said Lindy.

"Not bad," admitted Tony.

"It's an Afghan wolfhound," said Lindy.

Tony laughed.

"Don't you ever think of anything but animals, Lindy?" he asked.

Lindy smiled, and looked more closely at the girl.

"I know her," she said. "I think she was at school with me." She glanced at the name on the back of the photograph.

"'Alyss Spencer,'" she read out. "Yes, that's the girl. But she used to spell it 'Alice' when she was at school!"

"She's a hot favourite for the crown," said Tony.

"Well, I couldn't compete with glamour like that," said Lindy.

"But you will be coming to the ball, won't you?" asked Tony.

"I'll try to, if I've got time," answered Lindy. "But I can't hang around talking to you any longer, Tony. I've got to get out to the fair. Some of their animals need attention."

Lindy hurried off. After her visit to the fair, she made several more calls, then gave a hand at the kennels at the A.P.S. headquarters.

There was plenty of work to do, and it was the same every day. Lindy had another busy time on the day when the Carnival Ball was to be held. When she finally got back to the A.P.S. headquarters, Mr Green, the district inspector, had another job for her.

"Just one more call, Lindy," he said. "Will you go to this address? The woman there is worried about a dog."

Lindy drove off to the address she was given. The woman, a Mrs Bayley, was waiting for her.

"It's the dog next door," said Mrs Bayley. "I don't know whether I'm interfering, but the dog doesn't seem to be taken care of. The people are out all day, and the dog is left chained up. Most days they seem to forget to put out any food or water."

She led Lindy out into her back garden, and pointed over the wall.

"You can see it from here," she said.

A large dog was chained up in the next garden. The chain was short and the dog had little room to move. It lay there listlessly. Lindy could see no sign of food or water.

"It's an Afghan wolfhound!" she exclaimed.

"Yes," said Mrs Bayley. "Alyss Spencer bought it to swank around with, but she soon got tired of it."

"I suppose I'm trespassing if I go in that garden, but I'll risk it," said Lindy. "The dog needs attention."

Mrs Bayley got her a bowl of water, and Lindy went into the Spencers' garden. She spoke quietly to the dog and it gave a feeble wag of the tail. Lindy held out the bowl and the hound lapped greedily.

"Steady, boy," said Lindy. "Not too much at first."

The back door of the house opened. Alyss Spencer was back from work. With her was her sly brother Percy.

"What do you think you're doing?" snapped Alyss. She came closer. "Oh it's Lindy Martin! Well, you can clear out of our garden."

"Not until I've had a word with you about this dog," said Lindy.

"What business is it of yours?" retorted Alyss.

"It's my job," said Lindy. "Do you know you could be fined for neglecting a dog like this?"

"Fined?" gasped Alyss.

"A dog this size needs plenty of exercise, and lots of food and water," said Lindy. "It's cruel to keep him cooped up like this."

"You don't really mean you're going to have us summonsed, do you?" said Alyss.

"I'm just giving you a warning," said Lindy. "If you look after the dog better in future, that'll be all right. I'll call round again in a couple of days to see how he is."

"We'll see he's all right," declared Percy. "There's no reason for you to worry. This needn't go any further. Just between ourselves, eh?"

"That depends," said Lindy. "Suppose you start doing something for the dog now?"

"But I want to get ready for the Carnival Ball," wailed Alyss.

"So do I," said Lindy, "but I'll give you a hand first to clean the dog and get him properly fed. When we've finished the dog will look as smart as he does in that photograph you had taken!"

The Snoopers.

SOME time later, Alyss and Percy sank into chairs in their living-room. Lindy had just driven off.

"My hands will never be the same again," wailed Alyss. "The dog looks twice as smart as I do!"

"Interfering little pest !" said Percy.

" I wish you'd never got the idea of photographing me with a dog," snapped Alyss.

" Well, you want to be Carnival Queen, don't you ?" said Percy. " It was a good photograph." He scowled.

" But it won't look so good if people hear about this dog business."

Alyss sat up.

" Lindy Martin said she was going to the Carnival Ball !"

" That's right," agreed Percy.

" Suppose she starts talking when she gets there ?" muttered Alyss. " If she tells tales about that dog, I'll never get chosen Carnival Queen !"

" Too true !" said Percy.

" Hurry up and get cleaned," said Alyss. " Then we'll go round to Lindy's house. I know where she lives."

" What good will that do ?" said Percy.

" We'll find some way of keeping her quiet," snapped Alyss. " Perhaps we can stop her from going to the Ball."

" Oh, all right !" grunted Percy.

It was dark when Alyss and Percy set out for Lindy's house. Percy drove them there in his ramshackle little car. Alyss was dressed to kill for the Carnival Ball, and powerful scent mingled with the oil fumes of Percy's car.

They left the car at the end of Lindy's road and approached the house cautiously. Lindy's little van was parked in the drive.

" Let's take a look round the back," muttered Alyss.

The curtains of the living-room were not drawn, and the two snoopers could see Lindy's mother and father sitting there. Lights behind bedroom curtains showed that Lindy was upstairs getting ready for the Carnival Ball.

" Now what do we do ?" muttered Percy. " Kidnap her or something ?"

" There must be some way," frowned Alyss. She peered into the dark garden. " What are those ? Cages ?"

" Looks like it," said Percy.

" Let's see," said Alyss.

She opened the gate and tiptoed into the garden. Several small cages stood on the lawn. Alyss got close to the bars.

" There seem to be some birds in here," she whispered. " Have you got a light ?"

Percy struck a match.

" Birds all right," he said. " It would keep her busy if we let them out."

He sniggered, then yelped as the match burnt his fingers.

" Light another one," said Alyss.

She peered at the birds in the dim glow of the flickering match.

" These aren't cagebirds," she muttered. " I can see a thrush, and that looks like a blackbird over there."

She heard a rustling from a cage set a little apart from the others, and she went over to it.

" There seems to be a dog in here," she said.

Percy struck a third match, and Alyss peered into the cage.

" It's curled up at the back," she said. " I can't see it properly, but it looks like a dog of some sort."

She stood up and her voice was triumphant.

" Now we've got Miss Lindy Martin !" she said.

"How do you mean ?" asked Percy.

" Don't be dim !" snapped Alyss. " How can she accuse us of cruelty now ? She's got wild birds and a dog shut up in cages ! She gave us a lecture, and yet she behaves worse herself !"

" Gosh, yes !" said Percy.

" If she keeps quiet about our dog, we'll keep quiet about the way she treats her pets !" said Alyss. She opened the gate. " Let's go round to the front door and tell her so !"

The Carnival Ball.

 HEN they reached the road, Alyss and Percy saw a young man knocking on the door of Lindy's house. It was Tony Richardson, Lindy's student friend.

The door was opened by a girl in a gay dance dress. Her fair hair gleamed in the light.

" Is Lindy in ?" began Tony. He stopped and stared. " Gosh, it is Lindy !"

" I don't know whether that's a compliment or not," laughed Lindy.

" I came round to see if you were going to the Carnival Ball," said Tony.

" I'm almost ready. Come in," said Lindy.

Tony went inside, and the door closed. Alyss and Percy approached the house.

" We'll warn her now, before she gets a chance to talk to Tony Richardson !" said Alyss.

She banged on the door. Lindy opened it, and looked surprised to see Alyss and Percy.

" We'd like to talk to you," said Alyss.

" Come in," invited Lindy.

" This is private, said Alyss. She lowered her voice. " I just want to warn you that you'd better not tell any of the Carnival Queen judges about that dog of ours."

" What are you talking about ?" said Lindy, in astonishment.

" If you tell tales about our dog, I'll report you for keeping wild birds and a dog caged up in your garden !" snapped Alyss.

Lindy stared for a moment. Then she started to laugh.

" It's not a joke !" fumed Alyss. " I mean it !"

" You think I'm being cruel to the creatures I've got caged up ?" said Lindy.

" It wouldn't sound very nice if people were told how an A.P.S. girl treats her pets," said Percy.

" You'd better have a closer look at my pets," said Lindy. " Come on through into the garden."

Alyss and Percy looked doubtfully at each other.

" You've made an accusation," said Lindy. " Come and see how much truth there is in it."

Alyss hesitated, then stepped into the hall. Percy followed. Lindy led them through to the back door.

" Shan't be long," she called to Tony, who was in the living-room talking to her mother and father.

Lindy turned on a switch in the kitchen that brought into life a couple of lights that hung over the cages. When Alyss and Percy followed her down the garden they could clearly see the birds in the cages.

" Take a good look at them," she said.

" They're wild birds," said Alyss.

" That's a blackbird, and there's a thrush over there."

" The blackbird has got an injured leg, and the thrush has a broken wing," said Lindy. " I'm giving them treatment. They're safe in the cage until they're fit to look after themselves again."

There was a silence. But Alyss was not beaten yet.

" What about the dog ?" she demanded.

" You told me dogs should not be cooped up. Yet you've got one in a cage !"

Lindy went to the cage and opened it. The animal inside was curled up at the back.

" He's a bit sleepy," she said to Percy. " Fetch him out !"

Percy put his hand doubtfully into the cage and prodded. There was a sleepy snarl, then a wrinkled muzzle appeared in the doorway of the cage. Percy leapt back with a yell.

" It's a lion !" he shouted.

" A lion cub !" Lindy corrected. " It belongs to the Carnival Fair. It was off-colour and we were asked to treat it. Mr Green, our inspector, thought there might be trouble if it was kept with our ordinary animals at headquarters, so I brought it home and nursed it here." She shut the cage and smiled at Percy. " I think you'll agree that a lion, even a little one, has to be shut up !"

Percy swung round on Alyss.

" You and your ideas !" he snapped.

" What's wrong ?" called another voice. It was Tony Richardson. He had followed Lindy into the garden.

" Come on, Percy, I'm going home !" snapped Alyss.

She marched away, with Percy trailing after her.

" What's up with those two ?" asked Tony.

" I think you've just lost one contestant for the Carnival Queen competition, Tony !" said Lindy.

Alyss and Percy missed the highlight of the Ball, the crowning of the Carnival Queen. The band struck a chord and Tony Richardson stepped forward.

" Ladies and gentlemen, the judges have made a unanimous decision !" he announced. " The girl they have selected as this year's Carnival Queen is—Lindy Martin !"

Lindy gasped. Tony went to her to lead her on to the floor.

" But I didn't enter !" she protested.

" I entered you !" grinned Tony.

" But why choose me ?" exclaimed Lindy.

" The Carnival Queen needs qualities besides good looks," said Tony. " Charm, good humour, kindness. Your work with animals has shown you've got all those qualities, Lindy. Nobody could deserve the honour more !"

The tremendous applause as the crown was placed on Lindy's head showed beyond any doubt that everyone there agreed with Tony.

THE END.

PEOPLE and their PETS

Everyone knows "Mary had a little lamb"—but there was a real-life Mary, living in Ilfracombe, Devon, who had a lamb as a pet. Instead of following her to school, it used to go with her to the local chip shop. It loved chips, provided there was no vinegar on them!

The owner of a poultry farm in Cornwall seemed to be taking a chance when she adopted a fox as a pet. But Reynard and the 700 fowls on the farm became the best of friends.

"Hoi! Don't forget me!" For many years, this red squirrel paid regular visits to the home of a Northumberland lady. It arrived at the same time every morning and tapped on the window till it was invited in for breakfast.

Yoicks, tally-ho! This pet goat had an unusual "hobby"—running with the hounds when its owner went hunting in Georgia, U.S.A.

No wonder the boys on this New Zealand bathing beach are jealous. The girls are enjoying a ride on Opo, a very friendly dolphin of a few years back.

A lady in Los Angeles, California, kept a full-grown deer as a house pet. It slept in a bed, smoked cigarettes, and was especially fond of a cup of coffee!

This parrot used to sit in the doorway of a Dundee shop, and unsuspecting passers-by were often given quite a scare by its clever imitations of traffic noises.

Light-hearted stories often featured young girls who had unusual pets. This example from 1969 told the story of Sally, who found herself with a very strange companion – a performing seal.

SALLY AND HER SEAL

HOW would you like to have a seal for a pet — a seal that can do all sorts of cute tricks? This is the story of Sally Wilson, an eleven-year-old schoolgirl, who became the proud owner of a performing seal. Here is how it came about —

HULLO! WHAT DOES THIS NOTICE SAY?

CHILDREN'S PETS CONTEST
TO BE HELD IN THE
CITY HALL
ON SATURDAY
ENTRIES UP TO THE TIME OF COMPETITION AT 10 A.M.
Grand Prizes —
TO BE PRESENTED BY HIS WORSHIP, THE MAYOR MR. H. MOORE

A PET CONTEST. GOSH! THAT WOULD BE GREAT! I WISH MUM WOULD CHANGE HER MIND ABOUT LETTING ME HAVE A PET. PERHAPS IF I ASK HER ONCE AGAIN —

— BUT WHY CAN'T I HAVE A PUPPY, MUM?

BECAUSE THEY'RE DESTRUCTIVE LITTLE BEASTS, ALWAYS CHEWING UP SLIPPERS AND HOWLING THEIR HEADS OFF — THAT'S WHY!

MAYBE A LITTLE KITTEN, THEN?

NO! I'VE TOLD YOU A HUNDRED TIMES, I'M HAVING NO IDLE ANIMALS LOAFING AROUND MY HOUSE, EATING UP FOOD AND DOING NOTHING TO EARN IT.

A CAT'S USEFUL FOR GETTING RID OF MICE, BUT WE HAVEN'T GOT ANY MICE! IF YOU CAN FIND AN ANIMAL THAT CAN DO SOMETHING USEFUL, I MIGHT CONSIDER LETTING YOU HAVE A PET.

LATER —

THERE'S ALL THE PEOPLE GOING TO THE PET CONTEST. IT'S NOT FAIR, THEM HAVING PETS AND ME NOT!

IT'S A PITY YOU DON'T HAVE A PET, SALLY. BUT YOU CAN COME AND SEE "RAGS" WINNING THE CUP.

WHAT'S THE MATTER, SALLY? WHY ARE YOU LOOKING SO FED-UP? ARE YOU NOT COMING TO THE SHOW?

But Sally was in no mood for her friends' cheerful banter. The sight of all the happy boys and girls with their pets only made her feel worse, so she gloomily wandered away down to the beach to play with her ball.

IT'S NO USE. MUM WON'T LET ME HAVE A PET. I'LL JUST HAVE TO FORGET ALL ABOUT IT.

I'LL HAVE FUN WITH MY NEW BALL INSTEAD.

OH, DEAR! IT'S GONE RIGHT OVER THE BREAKWATER! I'LL HAVE TO CLIMB OVER AND GET IT BACK. GOOD JOB THE TIDE'S OUT.

WHA-? THE BALL'S BOUNCING UP AND DOWN IN MID-AIR! WHAT ON EARTH'S GOING ON?

WELL, I NEVER! IT'S A SEAL! IT'S BOUNCING MY BALL UP AND DOWN ON THE END OF ITS NOSE!

OI! THAT'S MY BALL. GIVE IT BACK TO ME!

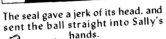

The seal gave a jerk of its head, and sent the ball straight into Sally's hands.

OH, GOLLY! IT'S FOLLOWING ME!

IT'S NO USE SHOWING OFF - YOU CAN'T COME WITH ME. GO AWAY!

IT'S STILL FOLLOWING ME. THIS IS AWFUL! I DON'T WANT A SEAL CHASING ME THROUGH TOWN.

Sally ran, and, almost as if it thought she was playing a game with it, the seal gleefully followed the girl!

Suddenly Sally felt something cold and wet pushing the ball out of her hand!

And could you blame her? But Sally managed to have lots of fun with her flippered friend.

A friend to all – that was Katy O'Connor. The cheerful Irish nurse would even change her appearance to help her patients – as this story from 1963 shows.

Suddenly one of the stewards appeared—

YOU'D BETTER COME QUICKLY, NURSE! YOUNG DEBBIE HAS HAD A SERIOUS ACCIDENT SHE TRIED TO DIVE OFF THE HIGH BOARD AND HIT HER HEAD ON THE BOTTOM OF THE POOL!

HOW AWFUL! SHE SHOULD NEVER HAVE BEEN THERE ON HER OWN!

I MUST OPERATE IMMEDIATELY, NURSE, THERE'S SOMETHING PRESSING ON HER BRAIN.

I HOPE SHE CAN STAND UP TO THE SHOCK, DR GRANT. SHE SEEMS VERY WEAK!

The operation appeared to be perfectly successful, but afterwards Debbie didn't recover as quickly as she should have.

MUMMY! I WANT TO SEE YOU! WHY DON'T YOU COME?

IF ONLY HER MOTHER WERE HERE! IT WOULD MAKE ALL THE DIFFERENCE TO HER RECOVERY

I HAVE AN IDEA THAT MIGHT HELP HER, DR GRANT IT CAN'T DO ANY HARM TO TRY, ANYWAY.

In the ship's hair-dressing salon—

I DON'T KNOW WHY YOU WANT DARK HAIR, NURSE. IT WAS BEAUTIFUL THE WAY IT WAS BEFORE!

I'VE GOT A GOOD ENOUGH REASON, STELLA. A CHILD'S LIFE DEPENDS ON IT!

I HARDLY RECOGNISED YOU, KATY. WHAT'S THE MEANING OF THE DYED HAIR?

I'VE GOT TO CONVINCE DEBBIE THAT I'M HER MOTHER. MAYBE THAT WAY SHE WILL GET BETTER QUICKLY!

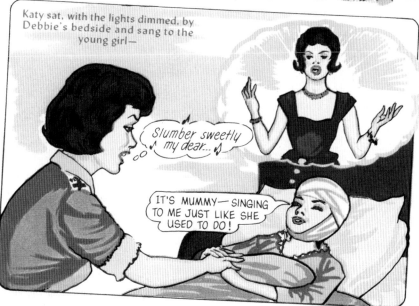

Katy sat, with the lights dimmed, by Debbie's bedside and sang to the young girl—

Slumber sweetly my dear...

IT'S MUMMY—SINGING TO ME JUST LIKE SHE USED TO DO!

The following day Debbie showed remarkable progress and soon she was as bright as usual. Miss Tomkins was so thankful that Debbie had recovered that she looked after her night and day. As for Katy— she spent her spare time in the hairdressers, trying to get her hair back to its normal colour!

Soon the Ventura docked at Cape Town—

GOODBYE, NURSE KATY. MUMMY HAS COME TO MEET ME. I KNEW EVERYTHING WOULD BE ALL RIGHT AFTER THAT LOVELY DREAM I HAD!

REMEMBER, NO MORE HIGH DIVING TRICKS FOR YOU, DEBBIE. CHEERIO!

THE END

Your Hat
THROUGH THE YEARS

1780-85

1825-30

1830-40

1840-50

1865-70

1870-80

1880-90

1920-25

1925-30

1931-40

1785-95

1805-10

1810-20

1850-55

1855-60

1860-65

1905-10

1910-12

1914-15

1940-45

1955-58

There are many classic stories advertised on this page, but read on to enjoy the start of one of the oddest ever to run in Bunty in almost fifty years.

The imagination of the Editor and his staff was certainly at its best when they came up with this thrilling adventure.

There were many months of
thrills and mystery before a happy ending was reached in this tale.

Stories from Madame Petrov's album appeared in Bunty for many years. This one, taken from an early Bunty Book, shows that the old woman wasn't beyond playing a trick or two to get results.

The DANCER from THE ISLES

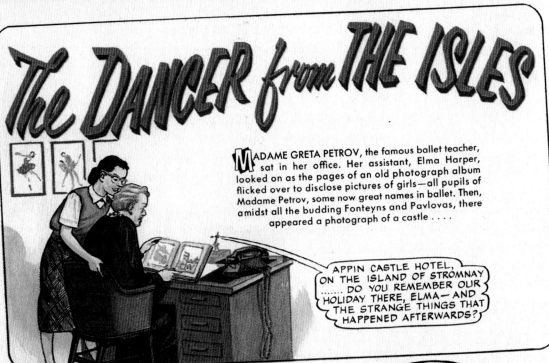

MADAME GRETA PETROV, the famous ballet teacher, sat in her office. Her assistant, Elma Harper, looked on as the pages of an old photograph album flicked over to disclose pictures of girls—all pupils of Madame Petrov, some now great names in ballet. Then, amidst all the budding Fonteyns and Pavlovas, there appeared a photograph of a castle . . . .

APPIN CASTLE HOTEL, ON THE ISLAND OF STROMNAY ...... DO YOU REMEMBER OUR HOLIDAY THERE, ELMA—AND THE STRANGE THINGS THAT HAPPENED AFTERWARDS?

THESE ISLANDS SHOW SCOTLAND AT ITS BEST........WHAT ON EARTH—? ELMA! LOOK AT THIS!

WE'RE GOING UP THE MOUNTAIN TO THAT COTTAGE, ELMA—I WANT TO FIND OUT HOW THAT GIRL LEARNED BALLET ON AN ISOLATED PLACE LIKE STROMNAY.

PHEW! THAT WAS SOME CLIMB, MADAME.

THAT'S THE COTTAGE......AND LISTEN! I CAN HEAR MUSIC— "SWAN LAKE"!

SHE HASN'T SEEN US. SHE HAS ROUGH EDGES, BUT THERE'S REAL **TALENT** IN HER DANCING — AND IT'S BEING WASTED HERE!

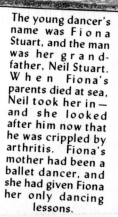

The young dancer's name was Fiona Stuart, and the man was her grand-father, Neil Stuart. When Fiona's parents died at sea, Neil took her in — and she looked after him now that he was crippled by arthritis. Fiona's mother had been a ballet dancer, and she had given Fiona her only dancing lessons.

COME BACK WITH ME TO MY BALLET SCHOOL IN LONDON, FIONA. I CAN OFFER YOU A SCHOLARSHIP TO STUDY THERE — AND THE CHANCE OF FAME, AS A BALLERINA.

I'D LOVE TO, MADAME PETROV — BUT I COULD NEVER LEAVE GRANDAD ON HIS OWN.

That seemed to be the end of the matter, until Madame Petrov's holiday was almost finished—

WHY, IT'S MR STUART.

I'VE COME TO TELL YOU THAT FIONA WILL BE READY TO LEAVE WITH YOU TOMORROW, IF YOUR OFFER STILL HOLDS GOOD.

OF COURSE IT DOES...... BUT CAN YOU MANAGE WITHOUT HER?

I'M NOT ALTOGETHER HELPLESS! I'LL GET BY — AND I'LL SEE THAT SHE'S READY FOR TOMORROW'S BOAT.

GRANDAD — WHERE WERE YOU? I'VE BEEN WORRIED.

I CAN LOOK AFTER MYSELF — AND I'M GOING TO, BECAUSE YOU LEAVE FOR LONDON TOMORROW! LISTEN.......

And so—

GOODBYE, LASS...... THE ISLAND WON'T BE THE SAME WITHOUT YOU — BUT I CAN'T LET YOU MISS A CHANCE LIKE THIS.

At the ballet school—

FIONA LOVES HER WORK. SHE'S GOING TO BE ONE OF OUR BEST PUPILS, ELMA.

GRANDAD SAYS HE'S GETTING ALONG FINE WITHOUT ME .... OH, I HOPE HE ISN'T KEEPING ANYTHING FROM ME. I HOPE HE'S ALL RIGHT.

Fiona made good progress in her first months at ballet school—but she would have improved even more if half her heart hadn't been on Stromnay, worrying about her grandfather. Madame Petrov was disappointed with her, and decided on an unusual course of action.

I'M ENTERING YOU FOR THE NOBLE AWARD, FIONA — IT'S A COMPETITION FOR JUNIOR PUPILS, AND IT CARRIES A PRIZE OF FORTY POUNDS AS WELL AS A SILVER CUP.

THAT WILL GIVE HER SOMETHING TO AIM AT — SOMETHING TO BRING OUT THE BEST IN HER.

But as the days passed—

NO, FIONA! YOU AREN'T CONCENTRATING!

I'M SORRY, MADAME .... PERHAPS I'M NOT CUT OUT TO BE A DANCER, AFTER ALL. MAYBE I SHOULD WITHDRAW FROM THE COMPETITION—

NONSENSE, FIONA!

NOW FIONA HAS **GOT** TO DO WELL IN THE COMPETITION, TO REGAIN HER CONFIDENCE. I'LL HAVE TO TRY DESPERATE MEASURES.

Next day, as the girls prepared to leave for the competition—

TELEGRAM FOR YOU, FIONA.

TELEGRAM

GRANDAD TAKEN ILL STOP! CAN YOU RAISE THIRTY POUNDS NURSING FEES STOP!

I DON'T KNOW WHO SENT THE TELEGRAM — BUT NOW I **NEED** THE NOBLE AWARD. I MUST REMEMBER **EVERYTHING** MADAME HAS TAUGHT ME!

SHE'S PUTTING ALL SHE'S GOT INTO THE VARIATION — AND SHE'S DANCING BEAUTIFULLY. THE FAKE TELEGRAM I MADE UP HAS DONE ITS WORK!

THE WINNER — A UNANIMOUS CHOICE, I MAY ADD — IS **FIONA STUART.**

I'VE DONE IT! OH, THANK GOODNESS!

As soon as the presentation was over, Madame Petrov went to the dressing-room. She wanted to explain her trick to Fiona, but—

FIONA STUART? SHE DIDN'T CHANGE — SHE JUST GRABBED HER CLOTHES AND RAN OUTSIDE.

Madame Petrov knew where Fiona had gone, and she rushed to a taxi.

EUSTON STATION — AND HURRY!

But the night train for Glasgow had left. Madame decided to follow Fiona to Stromnay, and two days later—

MADAME PETROV!

HOW CAN I EXPLAIN TO HER?

GRANDAD IS OUT OF DANGER NOW—HE RALLIED AS SOON AS HE SAW ME. THE STRANGE THING IS, NOBODY KNOWS WHO SENT ME THAT TELEGRAM.....

THEN MR STUART REALLY **WAS** ILL!

AMAZING, A REAL MIRACLE —THANK YOU, THANK YOU FOR MAKING ME SEND THAT TELEGRAM!

Fiona stayed to nurse her grandfather for two weeks more—and then her Noble Award prize money paid his fare to London, where Madame Petrov found rooms for him near the ballet school. The cottage on Stromnay was rented to holiday visitors, and Fiona became a day pupil.

FREE FROM WORRY ABOUT HER GRANDFATHER, FIONA WAS ONE OF MY FINEST PUPILS—AND NOW, SIX YEARS LATER, SHE'S MAKING BALLET HEADLINES!

THE DANGER FROM THE ISLES

FIONA STEWART

But dance wasn't always serious. This fun dance feature allowed the readers to make their very own national dancers.

The Dancing Dolls

HOW TO OPERATE THEM

First of all cut out the doll along with her shoes and the two bows.

Now pierce two holes at the black dots on the skirt and slip an elastic band through one hole, round the back of the doll and out the other, using the two bows to act as "stoppers"

Bend the shoes round, and fix them in position by pressing a small brass paper clip through the marked slits.

Put your first and second fingers down between the elastic band and the back of the puppet and fit them into the shoes. Now by moving your fingers you can make the doll dance.

WHAT BIRD BUILT THAT NEST ?

CRESTED CASSIQUE—The nest of this Mexican bird is made from grass and fibres.

TAILOR BIRD—This Indian bird sews large leaves together, using fibre as thread, and builds its nest inside.

HUMMING-BIRD—Strange horn-shaped nests like the one shown here are built by the humming-birds of Tropical America.

BLUE TIT—This bird's nest is common in Britain. It is made of grass and moss, lined with feathers, and usually built in a hole in a tree.

ALBATROSS—The nest of the albatross, a big sea-bird of the South Atlantic and South Pacific, is made of earth and usually contains only one egg which is laid before the nest is built.

SOCIABLE WEAVER-BIRD—Some African weaver-birds live in large colonies, building a giant nest in a single tree. Each family has its own entrance.

REED WARBLER—This nest is often seen built between tall reeds, on the banks of British rivers.

HORNBILL—Another Indian bird, which nests in a hole in a tree. The entrance to the hole is plastered up except for a small opening through which the bird hatching the eggs is fed by its mate.

CAPE PENDULINE TIT—This South African bird usually builds its nest around two or three slender twigs.

BOWER BIRD—This Australian bird builds a shelter of twigs over its nest.

WREN—the ball-shaped nest of the common wren is usually made from dried leaves, ferns, moss or grass.

SEA-SWIFT—You've heard of bird's-nest soup. The Chinese are very fond of it, and it is made from the nest of the sea-swift of Southern Asia.

OVEN-BIRD—The nests of the South American oven-birds are made of clay, and look something like native cooking-ovens.

The natural world was also central to this charming story, which started in the very first issue of Bunty. It combined factual information with the story of a young invalid girl, Molly, whose love of nature helped her struggle back to fitness.

They Gave It A Name

SALLY LUNN TEACAKES

In the eighteenth century, a young woman called Sally Lunn sold sweet teacakes, made from her own recipe, in the streets of Bath. An enterprising baker called Dalmer spotted Sally, bought her business and composed a song about her. His employees sang this song as they trundled their barrows through the streets selling the special teacakes.

JULIET CAP

William Shakespeare's famous play, "Romeo and Juliet," is set in Verona, Italy, and tells the love story of the son and daughter of the Montague and Capulet families, who are bitter enemies. Throughout the play, the heroine—Juliet—wears a net cap covered with brightly-coloured beads, which later became known as a Juliet cap.

GRANNY SMITH'S APPLES

Maria Ann Smith, an English immigrant, arrived in Australia a hundred years ago. Maria found some apple seeds inside a rotting barrel and planted them hopefully. Eventually, one of the seeds grew into a healthy young tree which bore fruit. Now this type of apple is grown in every corner of the world and is popularly known as Granny Smith's.

PEACH MELBA

This delicious dessert of peaches, vanilla syrup, ice cream and crushed raspberries was concocted by the famous French chef, Escoffier, in honour of Dame Nellie Melba. Dame Melba was an Australian opera singer, born in Melbourne in 1859. Escoffier greatly admired the famous singer and making this sweet was his way of paying tribute to her.

Another cartoon character who amused Bunty readers was *Mighty Mo*. A sort of female *Desperate Dan*, Mo was a mighty tough young lady – even when she tried to be sweet and pretty.

Lady Cyclists

Almost every girl loved fashion – and her bike – so this pictorial history of cycling was sure to appeal. Some of the outfits are amazing – although the bikes look more than a little uncomfortable.

Most women were unable to manage the two-wheeled cycle, but the appearance of the tricycle led to an increase in the popularity of the sport.

Two-seater tricycles then appeared on the market, on which the riders sat side by side. They were heavy and slow.

Many weird machines were invented during the years that followed. This one was called a quadricycle (it had four wheels).

The tandem tricycle of 1887 was quite a different proposition. It was a light, yet strong construction and the riders could hit up fair speeds on it.

At the end of the 19th century came the discovery that revolutionised cycling—the pneumatic tyre, which did away with sickening jolts and bumps.

This tandem was frequently to be seen on the roads about 1890, but proved dangerous due to the difficulty in steering it.

Now women began to take up cycling seriously. It became fashionable, and when titled ladies took to it, they were copied by the youngsters.

The dress of the women of those days was far from suitable for cycling, but fashion designers set about the problem and the divided skirt was the result.

The dress of the modern girl cyclist presents a rather startling contrast with that of the female rider of sixty years ago.

Touring by tandem has been gaining popularity during recent years. Tandems are not nearly as heavy as they look, and they can reach fair speeds.

Could Margie splash her way to success? Of course she could.

Strike A Chord!

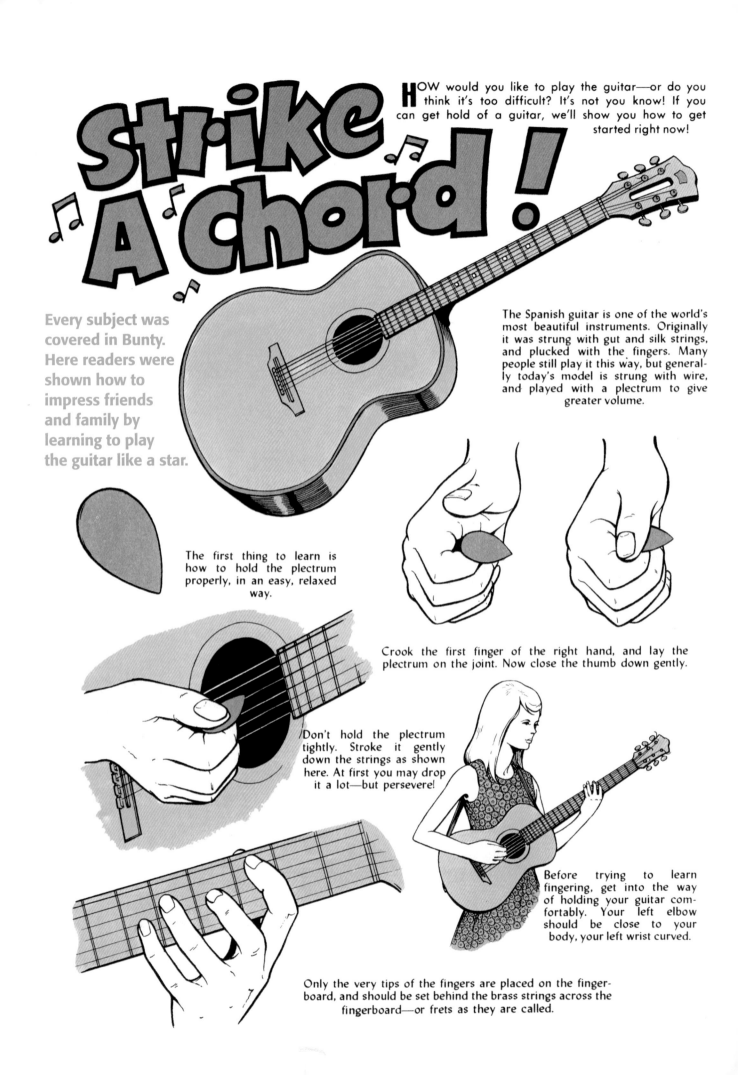

HOW would you like to play the guitar—or do you think it's too difficult? It's not you know! If you can get hold of a guitar, we'll show you how to get started right now!

Every subject was covered in Bunty. Here readers were shown how to impress friends and family by learning to play the guitar like a star.

The Spanish guitar is one of the world's most beautiful instruments. Originally it was strung with gut and silk strings, and plucked with the fingers. Many people still play it this way, but generally today's model is strung with wire, and played with a plectrum to give greater volume.

The first thing to learn is how to hold the plectrum properly, in an easy, relaxed way.

Crook the first finger of the right hand, and lay the plectrum on the joint. Now close the thumb down gently.

Don't hold the plectrum tightly. Stroke it gently down the strings as shown here. At first you may drop it a lot—but persevere!

Before trying to learn fingering, get into the way of holding your guitar comfortably. Your left elbow should be close to your body, your left wrist curved.

Only the very tips of the fingers are placed on the fingerboard, and should be set behind the brass strings across the fingerboard—or frets as they are called.

Here's one way to tune your guitar. The diagram shows the notes on the piano, which correspond to the strings of the guitar. Adjust the strings of the guitar until both notes sound the same.

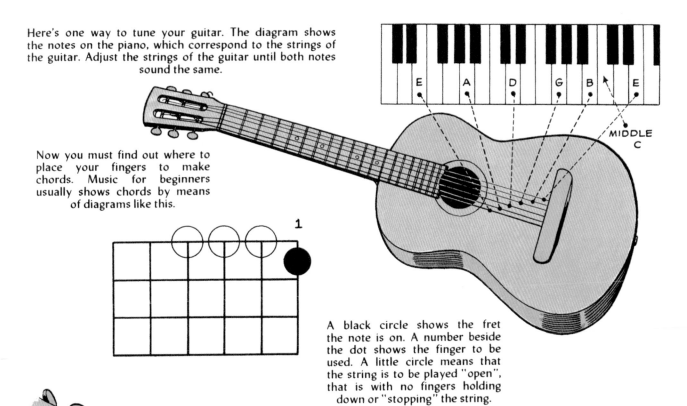

Now you must find out where to place your fingers to make chords. Music for beginners usually shows chords by means of diagrams like this.

A black circle shows the fret the note is on. A number beside the dot shows the finger to be used. A little circle means that the string is to be played "open", that is with no fingers holding down or "stopping" the string.

The chord shown is therefore played, by holding the first string down between the first and second frets, with the first finger of the left hand.

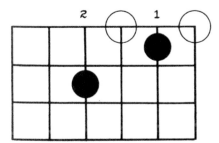

Now try playing this second chord. Hold the second string down between the first and second frets, with the first finger, and hold the fourth string down between the second and third frets, with the third finger. Practise playing both chords over and over again, changing from one to another. Strum with the plectrum held loosely in the right hand.

Go on! Have a go.

So there you are! You have mastered two chords which you will find can provide accompaniment to many songs. Easy wasn't it! If you feel you would like to learn more, buy yourself a book and carry on from there. Who knows! Some time soon, we may see you on TV—just like Nana Mouskouri!

A full page advertisement from 1965 promised great excitement for the following week. Some of the stories shown here went on to become huge favourites – not least the one shown on the following pages.

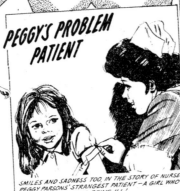

Meet "Z"—prettiest and toughest agent in Britain's Secret Service.

Like a bat in the darkness the girl soared towards the window.

MOST INTERESTING! SOMETHING I'VE NEVER SEEN BEFORE.

NOW I CAN MAKE MY REPORT.

Suddenly—

THERE'S SOMEONE AT THE WINDOW, GORDON!

TIME TO GO. BUT I SAW QUITE A LOT.

I'VE GOT TO GET THIS INFORMATION TO LONDON HEADQUARTERS AT ONCE!

I HOPE THE CHIEF WILL STILL BE HERE.

The girl pressed a secret catch and a whole section of the warehouse wall swivelled round.

WELL, "Z", WHY HAVE YOU COME? IT IS DANGEROUS FOR YOU TO BE SEEN NEAR HERE.

THE MATTER IS URGENT. I'VE FOUND THE UKRONIAN SPY CENTRE, AND THEY HAVE A MACHINE NEVER BEFORE SEEN IN THIS COUNTRY.

Later—

2 MAY

THE CHIEF HAD TO CALL IN SCOTLAND YARD. THE JOB IS TOO BIG FOR THE "WATCHDOG" SECTION TO HANDLE ALONE.

I HOPE WE'RE IN TIME. I THINK THEY SAW ME AT THE WINDOW.

TOO LATE! THE CAFE'S GOING UP IN SMOKE!

THEY'VE BURNED IT DOWN TO DESTROY ALL THE EVIDENCE!

DANGER

"Z" was taken back to Scotland Yard. There she met her Chief, and a police Commissioner.

JUST WHAT IS THIS ALL ABOUT?

WE'LL TELL YOU AS MUCH AS WE CAN, COMMISSIONER.

OUR GROUP, "WATCHDOG", WAS SPECIALLY SET UP TO WATCH PEOPLE WHO MIGHT BE A DANGER TO BRITAIN. SPIES, FOR EXAMPLE. AGENT "Z" IS ONE OF OUR TOP EXPERTS. YOU SHOULD HEAR THE REST FROM HER.

I'VE BEEN TRACKING SOME UKRONIAN SPIES WHO HAVE BEEN SENDING AND RECEIVING MESSAGES WITH A SPECIAL TRANSMITTER. I TRACED THEIR SIGNALS TO THE "TEN PINS" CAFE. HERE IS A PLAN OF AS MUCH AS I COULD SEE IN THE TIME I WAS AT THE WINDOW.

A PLAN!

An expert was sent for.

DID YOU DO THIS? IT'S HIGHLY TECHNICAL.

OH, I HAVE WHAT IS CALLED A "PHOTOGRAPHIC MEMORY." ANYTHING I SEE I CAN REMEMBER EXACTLY.

THIS IS LIKE THE EQUIPMENT USED TO RECEIVE PICTURES FROM TELSTAR, BUT IT IS MUCH SMALLER AND HAS THINGS I DON'T UNDERSTAND. WE MUST SEE THE EQUIPMENT.

BUT IT MUST HAVE BEEN DESTROYED IN THE FIRE.

I'VE JUST SEEN THE MAN WHO WAS WORKING IN THE ROOM ABOVE THE CAFE— HE WENT PAST IN A CAR! I MUST FOLLOW HIM. I'LL USE THE HELICOPTER.

WHAT ARE YOU DOING? YOU'LL KILL YOURSELF!

DON'T WORRY ABOUT "Z", COMMISSIONER. SHE IS NO ORDINARY GIRL.

MY GOODNESS! SHE'S HEADING FOR THE HELICOPTER ON THE ROOF ACROSS THERE.

LEWIS BRO

Later—

I'VE LOST HIM! BUT I'LL PICK UP HIS TRAIL AGAIN. HE WON'T ESCAPE *THIS* WATCHDOG!

H14

A RECEIVER THAT MAY GET PICTURES FROM TELSTAR— THE SPIES WOULD NEVER DESTROY THAT. AND I'LL FIND IT, WHEREVER IT IS!

NEXT WEEK—" Z " makes a daring raid on the spies' headquarters.

A four-legged friend causes problems for Bunty's favourite two-legged pal.

Christmas was always celebrated in Bunty. This festive cover shows the great prizes that were on offer in a special Christmas competition.

COSY CORNER

Christmas time was also a good time for readers' letters. This Cosy Corner page includes a money-saving idea for making Christmas tags and some special Christmas memories. There is also an advertisement for the latest Bunty Library publication – which came complete with star pin up.

A holiday story, a funny joke, a photograph or anything you think would interest "Bunty" readers could win you one of the following prizes.

POSTAL ORDER, RECORD TOKEN, SKIPPING ROPE, NEEDLEWORK CASE, GLOVE PUPPETS.

The Editor will also be awarding an EXTRA SPECIAL PRIZE of a WRIST WATCH or VANITY CASE to the best letter printed each week.

But remember—your entry MUST be original.

Send the entry naming the prize you would prefer and also mentioning the two "Bunty" stories you like best to:-

"Cosy Corner", "Bunty", 20 Cathcart Street, Kentish Town, London, NW5 3BN.

Fire?

I was in bed recently with a very sore throat, so my mother sent for the doctor to come and see me. My little brother, who is three, was in the bedroom trying to cheer me up when the doctor came. The doctor examined my throat and said that I had inflamed tonsils. My little brother turned to Mum and said that we would have been better sending for the fire brigade if my throat was in flames.

Pamela Winston, Wolverhampton, wins a record token.

Shark's Teeth

My dad works as a captain on a ship and the last time he went away, I asked him to bring me back some shark's teeth. I expected him to bring me back some small teeth in a plastic bag, but to my surprise he brought me home the whole skull with the teeth still in it.

Sandra Dunbavin, Illminster, wins a prize.

Christmas Greetings

Five years ago, my sister Paula and her husband Barry emigrated to Australia after they were married. Last year, on Christmas morning, mum, dad and I were sitting in the lounge speaking about my sister and her husband and wondering what it was like spending Christmas in the blazing sunshine and having a picnic on the beach. Suddenly the doorbell rang and I went to answer it as we were expecting my grandparents. I was given a wonderful surprise when I answered the door because there on the doorstep were Paula and Barry. They had arrived in London airport that morning and had come to spend four weeks holiday with us. It was the best Christmas present we could ever have got. And this year, I am going to find out what it will be like spending Christmas in the blazing sunshine as mum, dad and I was going to spend Christmas in Australia with Paula and Barry. So while you shiver in the snow, I will be soaking up the sunshine.

Lucky you! Petta Harper, London, wins a glove puppet.

Crab Catcher

This is a photo of my father and I out catching crabs. It was very interesting watching all the crabs and I even saw a mother crab carrying a little one on her back.

Lesley Anne Claxton, Churchdown, wins her choice of prize.

Good Guides

This year, our Guide company decided to make soft toys for our local children's hospital. Before we began, we went along to the hospital and asked to see the matron. We told her what we wanted to do and asked if it would be allowed. She was delighted with our idea and told us that the gifts would be greatly appreciated. We have already made fluffy gonks, two golliwogs and six glove puppets. We hope to have a lot more and are looking forward to delivering them to the hospital on Christmas Eve.

For her good work, I think Carol Summers, Wolverton, deserves her prize of a record token.

CATS ARE NOT WELCOME!

WHY DO THE PEOPLE OF THE MINING VILLAGE OF BUCKWELL DETEST CATS SO MUCH? JULIE BRADSHAW FINDS SHE'S IN BIG TROUBLE WHEN SHE TAKES A STRAY INTO HER CARE, AND DETERMINES TO SOLVE THE MYSTERY. DON'T MISS

BUNTY LIBRARY Nº 140

NOW ON SALE

WITH A SUPER  DIANA ROSS COLOUR POP-PIC

to bring you some more Christmas cheer!

Indian Adventure

My parents went to work in India when they were first married, and I was born in a mission hospital in Assam. When I was older, I was sent to a boarding school in a nearby town. I used to travel to the school by aeroplane. At half-term, my parents came to the school and took me for a picnic down by the river. It was a beautiful day and we all enjoyed ourselves very much. When it was time for me to go back to school, it was beginning to get dark. We piled all our picnic things into the car and set off. About a mile down the road my mother spotted what she thought was a tree trunk lying in the middle of the road. My father stopped the car and switched his headlights on full and we saw not a fallen tree, but a black panther. When the lights of the car shone on to him, he took to his heels and dashed across the road into the thick bushes. I couldn't wait to get back to school to tell all my friends about my exciting day.

Miranda Thomson, London, wins a postal order.

Christmas Surprise

For a long time, I had wanted a puppy and I had a good idea that I would eventually get one for Christmas. On Christmas morning, I rushed down the stairs to open my present and to see whether or not I had received the longed-for puppy. Immediately, I spotted a large box under the tree and headed straight towards it. I looked in and could not keep the tears from my eyes when I found it was empty. All my other presents were wrapped up in Christmas paper and I knew that the puppy could not be in those. Just then my mother and father walked in and asked if I had found my surprise. I told them I had looked in the box, but it was empty. Just then, my mother gave a cry and pointed to her white fluffy slippers which were heating in front of the fire. I looked over, and there to my delight was a tiny white poodle all curled up inside mum's slippers, sound asleep. I named my puppy Fluffy, after mum's slippers where I first found him. He will be two this Christmas and I am looking forward to opening my presents with him this year as he just loves to play with paper.

What a lovely present! Ann Mitchell, Inverness, you win a needlework case.

Gift Tags

As pocket money does not seem to stretch very far at Christmas time, I would like to tell "Bunty" readers of a good way to save a few pence. If you have some old Christmas cards left from last year, cut out some of the shapes such as a snowman, a Christmas tree, an angel and so on. Make a small hole in one end of the shape and tie a piece of cord through it. Turn the paper over and print TO and FROM neatly on the back and you have some lovely Christmas labels, free of charge. If you want to make them look even more glamorous, you can spread a thin coating of glue on the coloured side and then sprinkle with some glitter. This is a good idea for your "special" gifts.

Laura Barton, Inverkeithing, wins a postal order for this good idea.

Giant Tree

A few years ago, mum and I were doing some last minute shopping on Christmas Eve and when we arrived home, discovered that we had forgotten to get a Christmas tree. Mum rushed down to the shops and found that all the big trees were sold out. She then bought two small trees thinking that she would tie them together to make a big one. When she got home she found that my father had brought three small trees with the same idea in mind. We eventually had a super big bushy Christmas tree which was really five smaller trees all tied together!

Jennifer Watson, Taunton, wins a record token for telling us of her tree.

Naughty Nina

My father's work takes him all over the world, and my mother, sister Angela and myself all travel with him. We recently spent two years in South Africa and while we were there, my mother bought Angela and me two Siamese kittens. I called my kitten Nina and Angela called hers Lucy. We grew very fond of our pets and were most upset when mummy told us that we were to move to Oslo in Norway, as we thought we would have to leave our pets behind.

However, Daddy told us that we could send them on ahead and the quarantine period would be up by the time we arrived in Oslo. We had to have the cats' photos taken for their "passports". The photographer arranged to come to our house to take the photos, instead of us having to take the cats into town. When the time came for the photos to be taken, Angela had Lucy all groomed and sitting patiently for her photo to be taken. I couldn't find Nina anywhere. I hunted all over the house for her and finally found her hiding in the vegetable box. She was covered in dirt and the ribbon I had tied round her neck was filthy. I hastily brushed her and took her into the dining-room to have her photo taken. She is normally a very affectionate and obedient cat, but I could not get her to sit for her photo. Every time I moved away, she jumped down off the table after me. In the end, she had her photo taken with me sitting under the table so that she wouldn't jump down. I felt a right fool, but the photos turned out really well so it was worth it.

Diana Gordon, Oslo, has chosen a needlework case

★ ★ ★ School Trip ★ ★ ★

Our school organises many trips to Europe and also to different places in England. Last year our Vice-Headmistress pinned a notice up on our notice board asking who would like to go on a school cruise. I was really interested and my friends and I decided we would ask our parents that evening. I was delighted to find that my parents agreed that I should be given the chance to go on the cruise and was allowed to put my name down for it. When the time came I could hardly believe that I was really on the coach taking us to Southampton dock where our ship, the s.s. Nevasa, was waiting to pick us up. Our dormitory was called Pellew and I shared it with twenty-three other girls. When we were crossing the Bay of Biscay, I felt awful and was very sea sick, but luckily it soon passed. Our first port of call was Cadiz in Spain. The weather was beautiful when we docked at lunch-time so we spent the afternoon on the beach. The next day we visited a doll factory and the art and pottery museum. The following day we set sail again and our next port of call was Agadir in Morocco. There I had a ride on a camel and bought many things from the market. The next day we sailed to a small volcanic island called Lozarote and stopped at Arrecife. We spent most of the time on the beach and visiting the shops. Three days later we sailed up the river Tagus to Lisbon in Portugal. Lisbon is a beautiful city with many lovely statues. One I particularly liked was a statue of Jesus which was built by women to commemorate the home-coming of their husbands. Lisbon was our last stop before we headed home.

Jayne Green, Birmingham, wins a postal order for this interesting letter. She also wins this week's star prize—a wrist watch, well done, Jane.

All I Want For Christmas

About two years ago, there was a heavy snowfall about two days before Christmas Day. I immediately went home and unearthed my sledge and dragged it up the nearest slope. I was having great fun careering down the hill until my sledge hit a stone. I was immediately thrown off and landed head first on the pavement. I was knocked out with the impact and when I finally woke up, I was in hospital. They kept me in overnight and as there was no real harm done, mum was allowed to take me home as it was Christmas Eve. When mum drew the car up at our house, my dad and brother were standing at the front door waiting for us. I was very touched, thinking that they must have been very worried about me. My illusions were suddenly shattered when I stepped from the car. They immediately burst into the song "All I want for Christmas is my two front teeth!" When I was thrown from the sledge and bumped my head, I also knocked out my two front teeth! Still, I thought it was very funny and we all had a good laugh.

What a good sport you are, Alison McKenzie, Bolton. You have won a postal order.

Unusual customs from around the world were seen as educational and amusing. These are from the back cover of Bunty's first ever Christmas issue.

A Merry Christmas
AROUND THE WORLD

In Holland, the children are given special sweet biscuits baked in the shape of the first letter of their Christian name. That's why "Ina" wishes she had been called "Wilhelmina"!

Danish boys and girls make short work of the rice porridge which is served at their Christmas dinner. There is one large almond in the porridge—it is said to bring good luck to the finder, who is also rewarded with a gift from the hostess.

In parts of Germany, a room in the house is locked up for a few days before Christmas. The children know that their presents are inside, so they can't be blamed for trying a bit of keyhole-peeping!

A bad girl's nightmare in Italy—where naughty children are warned that, instead of toys, they'll find nothing but a lump of coal in their stockings!

How do you like this Christmas "blind man's buff" from Mexico? Blindfolded children have great fun trying to break open a jar hanging from the rafters. The fun continues after the jar is smashed—it's full of sweets, you see!

On Christmas Eve in Belgium, boys and girls leave out a few carrots when they go to bed—a tit-bit for Santa's reindeer!

In some country districts of Russia, it's the custom to wait until the evening star appears before tucking in to the traditional meal. Too bad if it's so cloudy that the stars are hidden from sight, isn't it?

And the cut-out wardrobe didn't miss out on the festive fun either. There were always special party clothes for Bunty to wear.

BUNTY   Dec. 25, 1965

BUNTY'S CUT-OUT WARDROBE

Round the clock with BUNTY on Christmas Day

Wake up — it's present time!

CUT out the figure and the clothes — being careful to leave on the tabs — and dress Bunty for a happy Christmas Day.

SLIT ALONG DOTTED LINE →

7 o'clock — let's have a party!

11 o'clock — Off to church!

3-30 — A hike with Dad!

1-30 — Christmas dinner!

© D. C. THOMSON & CO., LTD., 1965.

Printed and Published in Great Britain by D. C. THOMSON & Co., Ltd.,

12 Fetter Lane, Fleet Street, London, E.C.4.

St Elmo's wasn't the only school featured in Bunty, as school stories were prominent throughout the magazine's life.

JANET'S JUNGLE SCHOOL

AFRICA
ASIA
AMERICA
AUSTRALIA
EUROPE

SCHOOL

Early stories focused on young teachers – like Janet Spence, who taught in Central Africa.

More traditional serials featured scholarship girls who attended very unusual schools.

PIP at PONY SCHOOL

...ip girl at ...ere horse ...nts were ...fit for her, ...jodhpurs. ...ooty girls ...le ally in ...f an earl.

Stella does her best to turn a film into a flop!

Stella at Stage School

GOSH! IT IS EXCITING HAVING THE FILM PEOPLE AT OUR SCHOOL. IT MEANS LOTS OF THE GIRLS COULD BE OFFERED ENGAGEMENTS AFTER BEING SEEN ON THE SCREEN.

STELLA MAY... School, bu... education was... that students f... Stella received t... a documentary...

The pupils at Wansdale School all look forward to the time when—

★ Bad news travels fast! ★

SCHOOL'S OUT!

CAROL BELLING and Ellie Lane, two senior pupils at Wansdale, were preparing to go home after a disco.

DAWN

HEY, CAROL! HOW ABOUT LETTIN' ME WALK YOU HOME?

In the later years, grittier, more realistic heroines appeared – such as the girls from Wansdale School and Redvale Comp.

The COMP

ONE November's day, twins Hayley and Becky Sinden were out shopping in Redvale with their mate, Laura Brady —

HEY, LOOK! THE SHOPS HAVE GOT THEIR DECORATIONS UP! IT'LL SOON BE CHRISTMAS!

I DO NOT!

YOU DO, TOO! YOU START WRITING OUT YOUR PRESSIE LIST!

NOT THAT SOON, HAYLEY! WE'VE ONLY JUST HAD HALF TERM!

MY SIS STARTS THINKING OF CHRISTMAS AS SOON AS THE SUMMER HOLS ARE OVER, LAURA!

IGNORE THEM, ELLIE!

FINE, NURSE.

With school educational tours and cruises becoming more and more popular, girls who couldn't take part might have felt left out – but not if they read Bunty. Thanks to stories like the one shown here, readers could escape with the friends from Ridmouth County Grammer School who were on their very own school tour.

The End

School wasn't central to this memorable story from the 1963 Bunty Book, but it does make the ideal setting for Doris and her dilemma.

A FANCY DRESS FOR Doris

DORIS CHARTERIS was in the Second Form at Bellemont School for Girls—a boarding school in the country. Each year there was a Fancy Dress Ball in the nearby village of Amersley, and everyone at the school was expected to attend . . . .

I know that cousin Harold has been to a lot of Fancy Dress Parades, and I wondered if you could send me a costume that he has worn.

JUST MY LUCK! I'VE SPENT ALL MY MONEY, AND I CAN'T ASK FOR ANY MORE THIS TERM. PERHAPS AUNTIE FLO WOULD HELP OUT, THOUGH!

A week later—

THERE'S A HUGE BOX HERE FOR YOU, DORIS. IT MUST BE THE PARCEL THAT YOU'RE EXPECTING!

BRING IT UP, JANE. I CAN'T WAIT TO SEE IT!

BUT I CAN'T POSSIBLY WEAR IT. IT'S FAR TOO SMALL!

I THINK YOUR AUNT'S FORGOTTEN THAT YOU'VE GROWN.

THERE'S NOTHING ELSE FOR IT BUT TO MISS THE BALL. MISS PEMBURY WILL BE FURIOUS IF SHE DISCOVERS, BUT HOW CAN I GO IF I HAVE NOTHING TO WEAR?

On the day of the ball –

'I'll hide in the shoe cupboard until everyone's gone.'

'Help! Get the police.'

'I'm getting out of here fast!'

'Just look at what's come in!.'

The **Four Marys**

MARY RADLEIGH
MARY SIMPSON
MARY FIELD
MARY COTTER

TOOTS

MIGHTY MO

Katy O'Connor

WE'VE almost reached the end of our look through the Bunty archives, and there have certainly been some memorable 'friends' featured on the pages of your favourite magazine over the years. From The Four Marys to Mighty Mo, these well-loved characters entertained and amused girls for nearly five decades. We hope your favourite has been included.

HANDY MANDY

TERRY AND The Terrible Twins

Sugar Plum Fairy –
"THE NUTCRACKER"

Leading role –
"THE SHADOW"

The fiancée –
"THE FAIRY'S KISS"

Title role –
"PERSEPHONE"

A young girl –
"LES RENDEZVOUS"

The girl –
"THE RAKE'S PROGRESS"

Puppet ballerina –
"PETROUCHKA"

Johanna –
"SWEENEY TODD"